Today is the first day of the rest of your life.

LIFE OUTREACH INTERNATIONAL

ALL THINGS
new

Today is the first day of the rest of your life.

31-DAY DEVOTIONAL

Contents

Preface

"And He who sits on the throne said, 'Behold, I am making all things new.'"
(Revelation 21:5, NASB)

everything you have come to know and love about James and Betty Robison and their guests on *LIFE TODAY* is contained in this 31-day devotional. Real-life stories you can relate to. Authenticity. Courage. Love. Grace. Examples of God at work in the world today, through trials and our triumphs, successes and mistakes.

These devotionals are from the hearts of women and men just like you who needed a fresh start in their lives or their thinking, who longed for renewal, whose encounter with Christ allowed them to lay hold of the Scripture:

"Therefore, if anyone is in Christ, he is a new creation; old things have passed away; behold, all things have become new."
(2 Corinthians 5:17, NKJV)

As you read these devotionals, open your heart to the promise that God has for you – *"to prosper you and not to harm you, plans to give you hope and a future"* (Jeremiah 29:11).

No matter where you have been, what you have done, how badly your heart has been broken, or how many times you have tried and failed to start over, God wants you to let go of your past to make way for your future.

He wants to – He can! – make all things in your life new. **Starting today!**

Living free

The Spirit of the Sovereign LORD *is on me, because the* LORD *has anointed me to proclaim good news to the poor. He has sent me to bind up the broken-hearted, to proclaim freedom for the captives and release from darkness for the prisoners . . .* (Isaiah 61:1)

In a Holiday Inn hotel room, a carpet cleaner named Milton Green said to me, "Would you sit in the chair? I need to pray for you. You are the most tormented man I've ever seen."

Milton got right in my face. He said, "Son, now you listen to me. I've dealt with people with serious problems, but I've been following you for years. You're the best preacher I've heard, but you're also the most tormented person I've ever seen. Son, there's been nights I couldn't even sleep because I'm hurting so badly for you. I'm hurting for you now. Do you understand that, boy? You're so tormented. I feel so sorry for you. So would you just get in this chair?"

I still can't believe I sat in that chair, but I knew he was right.

I remember it like yesterday. I sat down like a little boy. He walked circles around me, and he must have thought that authority was determined by level of volume because he was literally screaming at the devil, at every foul tormenting spirit, at lust, bondage, rejection, compulsion . . . he was yelling at everything.

I thought, *Dear God, I hope these walls are thick!* And I thought, *That man is talking to the devil and I'm the only one in the room.* And I feared, *God, what if my friends find out? What if the preachers find out?*

As he got through praying he sat down on the bed and said, "Do you feel better? Do you feel like something just lifted?"

And I said, "Milt, I don't feel anything."

He leaned forward and popped me on the knee. He said, "Son, it is over."

Two days later, I knew something had happened.

Suddenly, the Word of God came alive. The Bible became the Living Truth of God in my hands; it was being hidden in my heart.

I began to preach that God could set the captives free. We don't have to live in bondage. We don't have to live with the enemy walking over us and become like trampled ground. We can be beautiful, fruitful gardens, and that's what God wants for you.

Here is the chair. Will you get in it?

James Robison is the cohost of the *LIFE TODAY* television broadcast with his wife of over 50 years, Betty.

PRAYER

Lord, lift the yoke. Break every area of bondage and defeat. Take authority over my life. In Jesus' name.

FURTHER STUDY

Matthew 6:13; Luke 9:1; 2 Corinthians 12:9; Ephesians 6:11; James 4:7

Jesus turned my mourning into joy

You have turned my mourning into joyful dancing. You have taken away my clothes of mourning and clothed me with joy . . . (Psalm 30:11, NLT)

everyone who has walked this earth has experienced some form of heartache. For me, the deepest heartache I've ever experienced was the loss of my sweet daughter, Robin. During my grieving process, I had moments of silence and times when I wanted to scream, and even times when I wanted to throw something.

A close friend told me it was okay to scream or be angry, whatever it takes to release the healing of such a loss to our hearts. I've cried out to God and asked Him, "Why? Where do I go? What do I do?" I was vulnerable, but instead of allowing the enemy to come and kick me while I was down, I chose to let God have my heartache and carry my burden. Sometimes I try to pick it up again, but I hear His sweet reply, "I've got it, Betty."

To this day, I'm walking through the healing process, on a journey that I never wanted to be on. But now, more than ever, I know my Father is holding me in His arms. And every morning I draw from His well of mercy and grace as He comforts my heart.

I have learned that God's mercies are new each morning, and He will never leave us or forsake us.

You might ask, "Where was He in my situation?" To which I can quickly answer, right there by your side. God is holding our hearts and will continue to as long as we are breathing.

Stop each day and breathe in His love and grace. He is the breath of life that allows us to go forward. He will heal our broken hearts and turn tragedy into triumph!

Betty Robison cohosts *LIFE TODAY* with her husband, James. The Robisons are also founders of LIFE Outreach International, a worldwide ministry and missions organization.

PRAYER

Jesus, You are peace. You are my peace that surpasses all understanding. I lay all my cares and worries at Your feet. In the midst of busyness and the pressures of life, I need rest. You are rest. You are the place where I am restored. When my heart is overwhelmed, I know You are the only One who can set it free from the burdens that weigh it down. You turn my sorrow into joy. There is nothing and no one that compares to You.

FURTHER STUDY

Psalm 30:5; Psalm 30:11

A perfect match

"I have been crucified with Christ and I no longer live, but Christ lives in me. The life I now live in the body, I live by faith in the Son of God, who loved me and gave himself for me." (Galatians 2:20)

In late 2008, I was diagnosed with a very rare form of leukemia; it's called Philadelphia Chromosome Positive Acute Lymphoblastic Leukemia. I went down to the Cancer Center in Houston, Texas, but the number one cancer research doctor in the world looked at me on Christmas morning and said, "We've got worse news for you. The only cure for this kind of cancer is a bone marrow transplant."

When you're an illusionist, you know how things work. You know things are going on behind the scenes, and even magnificent things can get kind of boring. But God was getting ready to show me something that I couldn't explain.

This is what the doctor said, "The only thing that is going to save your life is a substitution of blood on your behalf by a perfect match."

Essentially he said, "We have to find somebody who matches you at the DNA level. It's not just a blood transfusion, it is a DNA pairing."

The doctors went to the National Marrow Donor database, and out of 10 million people who are currently registered, there was only one per-fect match for me; one person on planet Earth whose blood was perfect enough for me. This person was, by the way, a 19-year-old girl. They contacted my perfect match and asked if she would substitute her perfect blood into me.

The whole process took time, and it was very, very difficult. It was a fight for my life at one point. But they put this new blood inside of me, and now I stand here today 100 percent cancer-free as a result of the only perfect blood on planet Earth that could save me from my disease. When they look at my blood today, they see XX chromosomes; they see her. It is no longer me who lives, it is someone else who is living on the inside of me. The life that I now live, I live by faith.

My natural birthday is April 20th. My new birthday, the day that they put the perfect blood in my body – the new blood, the new life – was April 23rd. So literally on the third day, I was resurrected from the dead because of the only perfect blood on this planet that could save me from my disease.

Jim Munroe is an illusionist and author of *The Charlatan: The Skeptical, Mysterious, Supernatural True Story of a Christian Magician.*

PRAYER

Jesus, thank You for loving me enough to give Your life for me, redeeming my imperfect life with Your perfect blood. Because of You, I can live by faith and the promise of eternity.

FURTHER STUDY

John 3:1–8; Hebrews 9:14

Heaven is worth it

And the peace of God, which transcends all understanding, will guard your hearts and your minds in Christ Jesus. (Philippians 4:7)

my brother Ben had a heart condition called Hypertrophic Cardiomyopathy; he was diagnosed when he was 13 months old. Most people didn't even know he had it because he never focused on his condition. He focused on bringing joy to others and living every day to the fullest.

When Ben was four years old, he accepted Christ. It was that very month that he had a life-threatening seizure.

As he was being wheeled down the hall to ICU, he said to our mom, "Mom, look at that bright light."

He was actually being wheeled down a hall that was under construction, there was no light. Later Ben said that he didn't remember anything about a seizure or waking up in the hospital, only this bright light and an incredible peace that he couldn't describe. He believed it was an angel.

A few weeks before he died and went to heaven for the last time at the age of 18, Ben had another near-death experience. He found himself in the waiting room of heaven, and he felt this peace, this peace he couldn't describe.

Afterwards he would go out to the lake at night and sit on our dock to ask God questions: "Why am I here? Why did I come back? What's the purpose?"

I found him out on the dock one night and asked him to describe his experience in more detail to me. He said, "You know, I call it a dream, or a vision, but I really don't know what to call it, because I was awake. It was very real. And somehow I knew I was ready for something more important."

I asked him if he was happy that he woke up. He said, "I guess." Then he started crying really hard. He had tasted heaven and his life paled in comparison; and he was tired.

It was really hard for me to hear as a sister, but I told him that this life isn't our life. Our life is eternal. And this life is an opportunity to give back to God and other people.

Ben said, "I think you're right. I think God also let me have that peace so I wouldn't be afraid of dying, and so that I would know that heaven is worth it."

Ally Breedlove is the author of *When Will the Heaven Begin?* It is the story of her brother Ben, whose YouTube video about his experience of heaven went viral and changed an untold number of lives.

PRAYER

God, thank You for Your indescribable peace. Thank You for the promise of eternal life. Thank You for people like Ben Breedlove, whose lives are too short but whose impact on us is so great.

FURTHER STUDY

Matthew 7:21; John 14:27; 1 Timothy 6:12; 2 Thessalonians 3:16

Do you believe?

Now faith is confidence in what we hope for and assurance about what we do not see. (Hebrews 11:1)

many people want to see God turn something around, but actually settle halfway through a turn. We serve a God who is more than enough, and yet we settle for less than.

I was told I would never have children, and I felt myself start to settle on that as my lot in life. I thought, *Well, God, maybe it will happen, maybe it won't happen.* And I felt God say, "This is where you have to put into practice what you believe. Do you believe I'm the God that can turn around this situation?"

I did believe in God's transforming power, and so I started believing He had a miracle for me. But I thought that meant God would answer my prayer and we would become pregnant within the next month, because like all good women, I had a plan and God needed to fit with my plan.

But I got frustrated when He didn't. I said to Him, "God, You need to come through for me NOW."

Eventually I began to realize that this was the journey of putting into practice what I believed, not after all my dreams had come true. Did I actually believe that God was going to answer my heart's desire, even if I couldn't yet see results?

For five years I met people in waiting rooms I would never have met. God took me on a journey of getting my eyes off me and on to the people I came across on the journey. I met people who couldn't conceive and I had new empathy for them. I threw baby showers for every pregnant woman in our church because God told me: "Sow the seed you want to see in your own life."

Isaiah 54:1 says, *"Sing, barren woman,"* which is a turn-around action. When you're barren, you don't want to sing. But Scripture is telling us to do the thing that will turn our circumstances around. You can cry, or you can find a song in the midst of your barrenness.

God does things suddenly and God does things slowly, and for us it was a five-year slowly. Five years passed before we had a baby and we called her Hope, because we never gave up. We had a son a few years later, and they are two amazing gifts from God, two signs of God being able to turn anything around.

Charlotte Gambill is the author of *The Turnaround God: Discovering God's Transformational Power.*

PRAYER

God, I know that You can turn around any situation or circumstance. I believe You are going to turn this thing around for me, in Your way and Your timing. In the meantime, use this journey to strengthen me and my faith in You. Amen.

FURTHER STUDY

Isaiah 54:1; John 11

Run to Christ

"If you love Me, keep My commandments." (John 14:15, NKJV)

Jesus tells us if we love Him, we will do what He says. But most believers today don't know what Jesus said.

Jesus' commands aren't like the commands of the law; His commands reveal the will of God for any given moment in our life. Then they empower us with grace and faith to do the will of God in that moment.

In 2008, I found out my 20-year-old son had a very life-threatening form of cancer. As it was, the Lord worked miracles and my son had an incredible healing. But the night that I found out, I was totally devastated. I didn't know where to turn.

The Lord led me to read what Jesus said about anxiety, worry and fear:

"It is I, don't be afraid." (John 6:20)

Peace I leave with you; my peace I give you. I do not give to you as the world gives. Do not let your hearts be troubled and do not be afraid. (John 14:27)

Blessed are those who mourn for they will be comforted. (Matthew 5:4)

Who of you by worrying can add a single hour to your life? (Luke 12:25)

When we get in trouble, we run to our relatives, our friends or counselors, but we don't run to Christ, and we don't teach our children how to run to Christ.

In a church that I attend, a 15-year-old committed suicide. He was used to running to his grandpa every time he would get depressed or bullied. Then he moved away and he couldn't run to grandpa anymore, so he took his own life. Nobody ever taught him to run to Christ.

Now when my kids come to me for help I'll say, "It doesn't matter what Dad thinks. Let's see what Jesus thinks." We'll turn to the subject in the Bible and their eyes light up when they start to read what Jesus said about their questions. And they see that He is real and He has the answers.

The Bible tells us there is nothing we go through that Jesus hasn't already gone through. Christ said, "I'm lonely. I've been bullied. I've been persecuted!" And He says, "Come to Me first. Learn from Me." That's why the Bible is here: so we can learn from the Lord Jesus. He has answered everything. He has given us instruction as well as peace.

Steven Scott is the author of several books, including *The Greatest Words Ever Spoken*.

PRAYER

Lord, I run to You. With all of my hurts and all of my joys, I want to come to You first. Put the desire in my heart to study Your Word so that no matter what I face, Your answers are already there, written on the tablet of my heart.

FURTHER STUDY

John 14:26 NASB; Hebrews 4:15; 2 Thessalonians 3:16

A story of hope

"Be still, and know that I am God; I will be exalted among the nations, I will be exalted in the earth." (Psalm 46:10)

at the age of 28, I was prompted by the Holy Spirit to try out for the television show American Idol. I always thought that if I submitted my voice to God, He would do something with it. But one month before the audition my wife Sofia unexpectedly passed away.

It devastated me. I didn't even know if I wanted to audition anymore. But I also knew I wouldn't have a chance the next year because I would be past the age cutoff.

Little did I know that God was in the midst of writing a story, a story of hope that people could look at to find hope of their own.

Psalm 46:10 says, *"Be still, and know that I am God . . ."* During auditions I remember saying to God, "Okay, here I am. I'm still. I know You're God. But it is not helping!"

Finally I started studying that verse, and it literally said: *"Cease striving and know that I am God"* (NASB). Forcefully make yourself let go.

The Lord was teaching me that I had to let go, otherwise grief was going to bury me and I would never see the beautiful chapter ahead.

I literally pictured myself with a hammer, breaking my grip, and saying, "I refuse to let this be the last of me."

Had I hung on to the pain, the depression, the hopelessness I felt, I never would have seen the beautiful chapter ahead. I never would have walked onto that *American Idol* stage; I never would have remarried or had my beautiful son; I never would have started a foundation in Sofia's honor that gives food and shelter and hope to homeless families.

Sometimes we have to let go of what we thought was the best plan for our lives, to make room for the future and the hope that God has for us. God literally wants to make your today so good that you'll forget the pain of your past. God has done all the work on the cross; all you have to do is let go, and let your heart beat again.

Danny Gokey was the third-place finalist on season eight of *American Idol*. He is the author of *Hope in Front of Me*.

PRAYER

God, thank You for the hope You have given me for a brighter future. I refuse to let this be the last of me. Help me let go. Help me begin again.

FURTHER STUDY

Psalm 55:22; Jeremiah 29:11; Luke 22:42

Rejected by man, but not by God

"He came to his own people, and even they rejected him." (John 1:11, NLT)

as I look back on my life, the most devastating wounds I've received have been inflicted by God's people.

We have all been hurt. But when you are wounded by people you've come to love and trust and felt safe with, people you respected and looked up to within the family of God, those wounds go really deep.

My husband and I had been members of a church for 15 years. While in the process of searching for a new pastor, some members of the congregation decided my husband and I had too much power since we both held leadership positions in the church. Through some political maneuvering, a business meeting was called and my husband was removed from his leadership position. When they announced the vote to the congregation, the congregation applauded.

One of the dangers, when the church treats people badly, is thinking that rejection comes from God. Luckily my faith was strong. I knew God was not like that church, that even though the church had rejected us, we had not been rejected by Him.

But we experienced a similar hurt in a second church. And then I didn't go to church for a year.

What I've discovered about myself is that when I'm wounded, if I'm not careful, I tend to retaliate and wound back. So when you're wounded, you have to be very careful to guard your spirit and guard your reaction so that it doesn't turn into a vicious cycle of "you've hurt me, I'm going to hurt you back." Instead God calls us to forgive so that we can move forward.

The very day we left that second church, a phone call came that led to my husband getting involved in a church plant. And one year to the day of leaving that church, we were in this new church plant, which is where we are today.

I look back on my life and the wounds that God has allowed me to receive, and so many of them have redirected me. They have moved me out of this church into another one, from one phase of ministry into another. But if you're clinging to the past, He can't direct you in new paths. You can't go forward while looking in the rearview mirror. You have to embrace what God has for you, even if it is very different than what you planned.

Anne Graham Lotz is the author of *Wounded by God's People*. She is the daughter of the Reverend Billy Graham.

PRAYER

Lord, You know the hurts that I carry. Help me to forgive and move forward. Lord, You know the hurts that I have inflicted. Forgive me and show me where to make amends. Thank You, Lord, that even when we are rejected by Your people, we know we are still acceptable in Your sight. Amen.

FURTHER STUDY

Psalm 118:22–24; Luke 17:25; Hebrews 4:15

In times of grief

"[God] comforts us in all our troubles, so that we can comfort those in any trouble with the comfort we ourselves receive from God." (2 Corinthians 1:4)

I began my career as a journalist. I started writing drama-in-real-life stories, people attacked by grizzly bears and caught in blizzards and all this. And as I interviewed people, again and again I would hear:

I went through this trauma. I'm in the hospital. I'm trying to get well. It's bad enough, but frankly as I look back on it, the worst thing was the Christians who came to see me. The church made it worse. Because I'm lying there and I just want to get well, and some people come in and say, "God's punishing you. You must have done something wrong." The next person comes in and says, "Oh, no, it's not God, it's the devil! The devil is attacking you." The next person comes in and says, "It is not the devil, it's God, but not because He's punishing you. He has chosen you to be an example to others." I'm so confused, and all I want to do is just get well.

I went to the Bible and one of the first things I learned is our words don't usually help. That should have been a message in Job. Because his friends came for seven days and seven nights, they sat there and just grieved with him. And I think they were really good friends. That is, until they opened their mouths and all these neat little pious theories came out about why God did this. Because so many of the words we say, even those that are well-intentioned, come across wrong.

I've asked a lot of people, "Okay, these are things the church did wrong; who did it right?" And almost never do they say, "Oh, there was a theologian from this university who visited me." Often they don't even say their pastor. Usually it is somebody like a grandmother who sits by their side, who when they need a glass of water gets them a glass of water. It's that practical demonstration of love and comfort that people need.

Instead of trying to find the "right" words to say, we can simply be a presence, or we can ask, "What do you need?" and let that person tell you how best you can help. That's how we show God's love even more than words in a time like that.

So that's my primary message to the church in times of grief: be slow to speak.

Philip Yancey is the author of more than 20 books, including *Where Is God When It Hurts?* and *What's So Amazing About Grace?*

PRAYER

Lord, I long to comfort people in their time of grief. Thank You for reminding me that I'm not expected to have the right words, or any at all. Make me a comforting presence to those in need.

FURTHER STUDY

Exodus 4:10; Psalm 22–23; Job 1–42

All the ways He loves me

. . . Give thanks in all circumstances; for this is God's will for you in Christ Jesus. (1 Thessalonians 5:18)

When my sister was 18 months old, she was crushed by a service truck and killed in our farm driveway. My mom and I were standing outside at the back porch and watched it happen.

They say trauma jolts your memory, and for me, that is my first memory. So fear formed in me right from the beginning. I had an ulcer by the time I was seven; was cutting myself through my teen years. And by the time I went to university, I was experiencing full-blown anxiety attacks and was diagnosed with agoraphobia.

Then in 2009 a friend dared me, "Could you write down a list of 1000 things you love?"

Who is not going to take a dare? So I grabbed a pen and started to write.

Probably by the time I got between 70 and 100, all of a sudden it was like waking up, and slowing down.

We have six kids, we home school, we farm; my life is happening fast all of the time. I'm trying to get meals on the table and off the table and kids into books and chores done.

But leaving that gratitude journal out on the counter, and picking up a pen and writing, "The sun is shining today; there is a blue jay up in the tree," allowed me to slow down and see that the world was overflowing, that God can't contain all of His grace.

And it wasn't about the gifts – I started to see through the gifts and into the heart of the Giver. I realized that the Giver wants a relationship with each one of us. By writing out 1000 gifts, 1000 things I love, I was really writing all the ways He loves me.

When I started to write the gifts and see how much He loved me, my fears began to fall away. I found it impossible to be terrified at the same time that I was giving thanks.

Romans 8:32 has become a verse I live by: *"He who did not spare his own Son, but gave him up for us all – how will he not also, along with him, graciously give us all things?"* If God gave us Christ, if everything is from Him and through Him and to Him, the counting of 1000 gifts is really giving thanks for One – Christ alone.

Ann Voskamp is the author of the *New York Times* bestseller, *One Thousand Gifts*.

PRAYER

Gracious God, Loving Creator, Your mercies are new every morning. Thank You for the beauty all around us, from the sound of children laughing to the smell of dinner on the table. There is no end to the expression of Your love. Thank You for all the ways You show Your love to me.

FURTHER STUDY

Psalm 16:11 NASB; Romans 11:36; 1 John 4:18

A Father's love

For God so loved the world that He gave His only begotten Son, that whoever believes in Him should not perish but have everlasting life. (John 3:16, NKJV)

You learn about a father's love when you have a daughter.

I remember when my Jessica was three years old and fell sick with a viral attack. She was sick for several days with a high fever. I prayed, I rebuked, I cursed it out and prayed it in; I did everything I knew how. My heart, a father's heart, ached for her healing.

I remember going to my study, kneeling down, weeping and praying, "God, please. I've prayed; I've done everything I know how. I don't want to see her suffer."

I opened my Bible to Genesis 22:2, where it talks about Abraham offering his son Isaac, and I just got lost in the story.

God said, *Take now your son, your only son, the son that you love . . . and offer him on the mountain that I will show you.*

I began to see a picture of Christ. I was reminded that God offered His Son, His only Son, the Son that He loves. We'll never know how much God loves us until we know how much God loves Jesus, because He gave Jesus up for us.

When I read that, I was overwhelmed by the love of God. I began to see Jesus on the Cross, how He wept and cried and suffered for our forgiveness. And He called out, "My God, my God, why have You forsaken me?"

And I saw how Isaac carried the wood, just like Jesus carried the cross up that mount, and how God stopped Abraham from the pangs of killing his son. But God never spared Himself. When it came down to it, God didn't spare His own Son. God gave up the Son that He loved for me.

All of a sudden when I felt that love of God I began to weep; not because of my daughter, who was still crying in the other room, but because of God's love for me. And the moment I wept and felt God's love, her crying stopped. She had been crying for days, almost nonstop, and suddenly she was sound asleep, resting peacefully. And when she woke up she was completely well.

Joseph Prince, pastor from New Creation Church, Singapore, is the author of *The Power Of Right Believing*.

PRAYER

Father, I thank You. By not sparing Yourself or Your own Son, You've made me righteous in Christ. I pray that people worldwide will come to know the depth of Your love for us.

FURTHER STUDY

Genesis 22; Romans 5:19; 1 John 4:16–18

Heavenly ever after

Know therefore that the LORD *your God is God; he is the faithful God, keeping his covenant of love to a thousand generations of those who love him and keep his commandments.* (Deuteronomy 7:9)

In 2007, I was asked to write a book on raising up our sons to be godly husbands, preparing him for the other woman. Right before I went to turn it in, I got scared that a demonic attack would come on me and my family.

My son was a senior in high school at the time and I said, "Jake, you've been a privilege to raise. You've made me look really good as a mom. But you are going to move out when your senior year is over and I need to know up front, before I release a book on raising sons, are you going to rebel against God?"

He assured me his faith was strong, so I pushed send and we started doing mother/son conferences together.

In that time, my husband got a job that we had prayed for. We had really good boundaries in our marriage, but this job broke all those boundaries, and within three or four months we were separated.

When my son got the news, he walked away from the Lord and started using drugs and alcohol.

I had this moment where I fell to my knees and I said, "God, if You don't give me back my family, I don't want to be in the ministry anymore. I'm quitting."

I felt like the Lord said to me, "Was My death on the cross not enough for you to follow Me? Are you really going to judge Me by a man's actions?" And in that moment, God showed me that I needed to lay my Isaacs down. My family had become a god more than God, and that I needed not to let anybody, including my own husband, control my faith. So I laid down my happily-ever-after and started to live for heavenly-ever-after.

I realized that at the end of my life, even if I didn't get my husband back, even if my son never returned to the Lord, I would be the great-great-great grandmother who was remembered as a woman who loved and obeyed God in spite of everybody else's actions.

God showed me that everybody has a life they wanted or dreamed about, but the life I wanted means nothing compared to the legacy I'm going to leave when I'm known for following Christ.

Sheri Rose Shepherd, former Ms. United States, was one of the first guests on *LIFE TODAY*. She is the author of *Your Heart's Desire*.

PRAYER

God, life is hard right now, but You have trusted me with this pain and I trust You in it. I don't know what You're going to do with it, but Your will be done. Use it how You choose. Because I want to be remembered as someone who chose to follow You.

FURTHER STUDY

Genesis 22; Exodus 20:6; Psalm 78:1–8

The real miracle

"Which is easier, to say to the paralytic, 'Your sins are forgiven you,' or to say, 'Arise, take up your bed and walk'?" (Mark 2:9, NKJV)

In the middle of a brothel house, while I was ministering to sex slaves in India, a very elderly woman sat on the floor next to a wall of gods that the Indians worshipped. Through a translator, I talked to her about Jesus.

An angry woman entered the room and said, "You talk about Jesus? Show me your Jesus." Pointing at the woman on the floor she said, "This is my sister. She hasn't walked for four years. She hasn't stepped out of this house. We've been praying to our gods that she walks. If your God is real, make my sister walk. Make her walk."

So I started praying. I said, "God, You know I've seen blind people see, deaf people hear," and a dozen other miracles I've seen right in front of my eyes.

We prayed and we kept praying. And the first time she got up I felt bad because I saw the pain in her face as she tried to stretch out legs she hadn't used for four years. I had each of my friends on either side of her, but she couldn't put any pressure on her legs.

They sat her down in a chair. We prayed more. Then her face changed and she said, "I'm ready!"

She got up all by herself and started walking. Then she started jumping up and down. It was amazing!

Her sister went to the gods on the wall and thanked them. I said, "No, your gods are dead. This was Jesus Christ. Jesus is alive. This is the power of His blood. He is alive; the Most High God. He raised Himself from the dead, no one else did that. He was God in flesh."

I went back to my hotel and my friend said, "Do you know who that woman was that God healed?"

I said, "Who?"

He said, "Forty-five years ago that woman started that whole block of 150 brothel houses. She is personally responsible for thousands of girls who have been raped, killed, starved, beaten and forced into sex slavery. She was the one responsible, the madam of the madam of the madams."

Can you imagine all the evil she has caused? Yet Jesus still loves her enough to show His power to her. That is the real miracle.

If God can do this with her broken pieces, what can God do with yours?

Nick Vujicic has never let being born without arms or legs stop him from following the will of God. He is the author of books such as *Stand Strong*; *Unstoppable*; and *Life Without Limits*.

PRAYER

Lord God, You have given me the greatest miracle of all: To know You as my personal Lord and Savior and the gift of eternal life. Use me to be a miracle to someone else, bringing the Good News of Your Salvation to those in need.

FURTHER STUDY

Daniel 4:2–3; Isaiah 57:18; John 21:20–22

Open doors

Each of you should use whatever gift you have received to serve others, as faithful stewards of God's grace in its various forms. (1 Peter 4:10)

When I was seven years old, the Lord spoke to me and told me I would be a missionary in Africa. The unfolding of that call took nearly 20 years, but God's hand was evident in every step.

When I was 16 years old while attending a revival meeting in Pensacola, Florida, the evangelist invited a guest to speak. He said, "This woman is the head intercessor for Reinhard Bonnke." I'd never heard of Reinhard or this woman, but when she got up and began to pray, the Holy Spirit spoke to me very clearly, "You are going to work with the man that she talked about."

I went back to my room and wrote a letter to Reinhard, "The Lord spoke to me today. I'm supposed to work with you."

I got on the Internet and began to see pictures of millions of people gathered at crusades to hear Reinhard preach the Gospel. I realized this was a huge ministry and this guy would probably never get my letter. I still have that letter to this day. I never mailed it.

Seven years went by and, through a very strange turn of events, I ended up working for Reinhard's ministry. I was stocking shelves and sweeping floors in the warehouse. And I felt so happy! I felt like this was the fulfillment of what the Lord had spoken to me all those years earlier.

Then, out of the blue, Evangelist Reinhard Bonnke himself invited me to travel with him as an assistant, and we came to know one another. Little by little he started to give me ministry opportunities, and finally the day came when he said, "I believe that you're supposed to be the one to take this ministry into the next generation."

I never told Reinhard that I could preach, that I had planted churches, that I was called as a little boy to be a missionary, that I had written him a letter all those years ago. In fact, it never entered into my head that I could be the successor to Reinhard Bonnke until the words came out of his mouth.

I think if I would have pursued that role, the doors would probably have shut. But when we are faithful wherever we find ourselves – whether in the warehouse or on the platform – God will open doors.

It gives me confidence because whenever we're facing difficult times, I can say, "Lord, I didn't put myself here. You put me here, and Your grace is sufficient for me."

Daniel Kolenda, successor to Reinhard Bonnke in the Christ for All Nations ministry, is the author of Live Before You Die: Wake up to God's Will for Your Life.

PRAYER

Dear Father, thank You for the gifts You have given me and the dreams You have placed in my heart. I trust You to open doors for me in Your timing. And wherever You place me, be it the lowest position or the top, I will glorify You.

FURTHER STUDY

Proverbs 18:16 NASB; Isaiah 55:8; 2 Corinthians 12:9

My way, or God's way?

And what does the LORD require of you? To act justly and to love mercy and to walk humbly with your God. (Micah 6:8)

ministering to women in prison is not the vision I had for my life. When the Lord found me and gave me this vision, I was kicking and screaming the whole way. But, like the Israelites, after wandering around in circles for 40 years, I finally said, "Okay, Lord, I'll do it."

So I went to a work release center in Birmingham, Alabama and started ministering. And I loved it! It was like having grandchildren. I would go in, love them, and then leave.

But while I was ministering, I found that prison is like a revolving door; when the women were released, they just came right back.

I thought, "Well, I can do better than this."

So I badgered the state of Alabama, "Give me some women!"

And they said, "What do you know?"

I said, "Only that God has put it on my heart to do more than these work release centers."

By the time the women were scheduled to arrive, I moved out of my home and arranged it in a great way for them. You see, I was doing it the "Brenda way" still. I wasn't going to get my hands dirty. I had a house mom and a driver and a cook. I was going to love them from a distance, like grandchildren, and every once in a while I envisioned going by and teaching them, loving on them, and then I would fly right on out.

To make a long story short, the State sent me the roughest women they could find, and within the hour my housemother quit and I realized I wasn't playing church anymore. When I cried out to God in those dark times, the Lovelady Center was what He had in mind for me.

Many times I wanted to give up. I cried out to God, "Lord, You've made a mistake. This is not what I signed on for." But I knew I was where God wanted me to be.

The Lord brought my seven women, then 40, then 400. Thousands of women have been through the program, and Shay, my very first lovely lady, now works for the Lovelady Center as Director of Intake.

At some point you have to decide, are you going to do things your way, or God's way? It's not in me to disobey Him anymore. I did that for too many years. Now whatever He says, I do with everything in me.

Brenda Spahn is the founder of the Lovelady Center, ministering to women released from prison, and the author of *Miss Brenda and the Loveladies.*

PRAYER

Lord, I humbly submit the vision I have for my life and embrace the higher calling that You have planned. Wherever You want me to go, I will go. Whatever You want me to do, I will do. I want Your will for my life.

FURTHER STUDY

1 Kings 2:3; Proverbs 16:3; Isaiah 48:17; 2 John 1:6

Created for more

As a prisoner for the LORD, then, I urge you to live a life worthy of the calling you have received. (Ephesians 4:1)

after working in ministry with my husband, then becoming a full-time stay-at-home mom, I started to ask God, "Is there something more? Are there certain assignments that are for me alone? Are there gifts that You put in me when You knit me in my mother's womb – things that make me come alive?"

Right around the same time, we moved to New York. Within four months I started having panic attacks. I had them on trains, elevators, subways and in crowds. Have you ever been to New York? It's really impossible to avoid these things.

After 18 months of this, my husband said we didn't have to stay in New York. And that act of surrender was enough to give me room to ask, "Is there something that God is working out in me?"

I asked Christ into my life and my heart at a young age, but had never known what it meant to utterly depend on Him for strength until September 20, 2011. I woke up at 3 a.m. in a panic, like I did so many times before, but this time I cried out, "Rescue me Jesus! Deliver me. I cannot do this without You." And for the first time, I experienced brokenness and being rebuilt.

In the weeks that followed, I began to see brokenness in people all around me. I started reading the work of Victor Frankl, Holocaust survivor, who says that the root of anxiety is unfulfilled responsibility, which basically means you know you're made for something and you're not doing it.

This was precisely what I was wrestling with when we came to New York: "Was I created for more?"

Women often get lost in our roles and we confuse our roles for our calling. Actually, our roles enhance our calling. But a calling is when your talents and your burdens collide.

Talents are those birthright gifts that made you come alive when you were not quite a teenager. Burdens are what keep you up at night, what make you weep.

Burden for me is people waking to the giftings God puts in their hearts and recognizing that in order to have a calling you must have a Caller.

I believe that calling is for everyone, male and female. I believe that if we are sitting at His feet and we say, "God, what is it that You're doing? Just put me to work," He will.

Rebekah Lyons is the author of *Freefall to Fly*.

PRAYER

God, what is it that You're doing? Where is Your hand moving in the world? Put me to work. Just give me Your marching orders. You know what part of the body I'm supposed to be, so show me what that is and make the need great right in front of me so that I can be fully present to the burden You have put on my heart.

FURTHER STUDY

Psalm 139:13; Romans 8:28; Ephesians 2:10

An imprint like no other

"Before I formed you in the womb I knew you, before you were born I set you apart; I appointed you as a prophet to the nations." (Jeremiah 1:5)

my dad was a detective with the Dallas Police Department. I can remember being about 10 years old when he took me to the department to be fingerprinted.

I looked up at him and asked, "Dad, why do you fingerprint people?"

He said, "Well, to identify them at the scene of a crime."

I remember asking him this question: "Is that why we have a fingerprint? So we can be identified for something wrong that we've done?"

And my dad really didn't have an answer for me. He said, "That's just what I do, son."

Four years later, sitting in church, our pastor said, "Look at your hand." He said, "Did you know that you have a fingerprint that nobody else has?"

Of course I knew it, but that was the first time I can remember, at 14 years of age, when God spoke to me. He said, "This is so you can leave an imprint that nobody else can leave."

Up to this point, the only thing forensic scientists had known to do with a fingerprint was to identify someone who committed a crime. But that day in that church, the Lord spoke to me the real reason for fingerprints:

God has given us this fingerprint that nobody else has, and that nobody has ever had in history, that nobody in the future will ever have, so that we can leave an imprint in the world that nobody else can leave.

We go through life longing for significance. There's something on the inside of every one of us that thinks, *I was made for more.* And yet, literally at the end of our fingertips is this fingerprint that is so unique that nobody in history has ever had it, and nobody in the future ever will. You may think you are ordinary, with nothing to distinguish you from everyone else. But all you have to do is look at your fingertip and there's that reminder.

Keith Craft is the pastor of Elevate Life Church and author of *Your Divine Fingerprint: The Force that Makes You Unstoppable.*

PRAYER

God, thank You for loving me so much that You created me unlike all others. Your Word says You know the number of hairs on my head, so of course You would recognize my unique fingerprint. Lead me Lord, in the ways everlasting, that I may come to realize the imprint You designed for me to leave in this world that nobody else can.

FURTHER STUDY

Luke 12:6–7; John 17:20–23

Be you

And we all, who with unveiled faces contemplate the LORD's glory, are being transformed into his image with ever-increasing glory, which comes from the LORD, who is the Spirit. (2 Corinthians 3:18)

One of the core issues that every woman struggles with is identity. *Who am I? Who am I supposed to be?*

And then God comes and says, "You're supposed to be you. You are the only one who gets to be you. You are the best you there ever was! I made you and all of your quirky uniqueness and qualities on purpose."

Jesus is the only One who is perfect; we're not ever going to be perfect. That's okay, actually. He's grace for our humanity. But we are invited to go on this journey with Him, deeper into His heart. Because when we come to know the love of Jesus more profoundly, the more true to ourselves we become. And we actually start to like that person.

The message given to women, particularly in Western countries, is "the less you weigh, the more value you have," and it's because of the way we bear the image of God. Women bear the image of God primarily through our essence and our beauty; it's more than our external beauty, but women seem to make it known that way more often. So women have been targeted throughout time, history and nations, with hatred from the enemy who fiercely wants to destroy that image.

But the thing about women and the assault on our beauty is that it translates into an assault on who we are as women – our personalities, our giftings. We're terrified that who we are is not enough, and certainly the messages throughout our lives have told us that that's not enough. But there's healing available, and I'm after that. Because the truth is, the only reflection that really matters is the one I see in God's eyes.

Becoming myself is a journey into the woman that God created me to be. And we're all on that journey, because God says we are being transformed into the very image of Christ. And I want to cooperate with Him in that process.

We have to stop basing our identity and how we feel about ourselves on our looks, our weight, our past, our failure, our sin, and begin to step into the full work of Christ and who He says we are. So go ahead and be you. Be the one God created you to be, the one He intended when He dreamed of you.

Stasi Eldredge is the author of *Becoming Myself: Embracing God's Dream of You.*

PRAYER

God, help me overcome my need to be beautiful by the world's standards, so that I can come to see my worth and value and beauty through Your eyes. Help me embrace the person You purposefully created me to be.

FURTHER STUDY

Genesis 1:27; Romans 8:29; Romans 12:2; 2 Corinthians 4:16–18

Desired by God

Your adornment must not be merely external – braiding the hair, and wearing gold jewelry, or putting on dresses; but let it be the hidden person of the heart, with the imperishable quality of a gentle and quiet spirit, which is precious in the sight of God. (1 Peter 3:3–4, NASB)

Growing up, I was like all young girls – I wanted to be desired. But these young girls, they're looking to the world to call them beautiful. And that's where I was when I got involved in modeling. I was looking to the world to tell me I was beautiful, accepted, worthy.

One of the things that really drove me was seeing models in magazines, television shows and advertisements. I remember thinking that models had it made. The world calls them beautiful; the world says they're important. They're happy, successful, they have money and men flock to them.

But the truth is the night I was crowned a Victoria's Secret Runway Angel was one of the most insecure nights of my life.

I'd known for years that a big part of the industry was selling sex – teasing and tempting men – but the epiphany didn't hit until a photographer yelled at me, "This is what you get paid for!" There was only one type of woman I knew who sold sex for a living, and I didn't want to be her.

I left modeling, and since then God has really put on my heart this crazy passion to share with girls about all of the pressures that the media places on them. They need to know that the images they see are an illusion. There is nothing real about them.

One in five females now has an eating disorder, and it is showing up in girls who are younger and younger. My own cousin, at eight years of age, told me she wanted to learn to throw up her food so she could be pretty like me. It broke my heart. And I believe the images of models in magazines, the ones women and girls feel like they have to compare themselves to, are a huge contributor. Unfortunately, some of the images that I used to take put that kind of pressure on young girls and women too.

What young girls don't realize is that we have an amazing God in heaven who desires us. My husband definitely makes me feel beautiful, but I know the reason he looks at me that way is because that's how Christ looks at me. Christ is not concerned with our outer appearance; He looks at the beauty of our heart.

Kylie Bisutti is a former Victoria's Secret runway model and the author of *I'm No Angel.*

PRAYER

Lord, more than outward beauty, I desire to have a beautiful heart. Thank You for loving me, for desiring me. I pray that everyone would know the depth of Your love, which has nothing to do with the clothes that we wear, the size of our hips, or the clarity of our skin. Amen.

FURTHER STUDY

1 Samuel 16:7; Matthew 23:27; 1 Timothy 2:9–10

Without Him there is nothing

I would have despaired unless I had believed that I would see the goodness of the LORD In the land of the living. (Psalm 27:13, NASB)

i started writing songs in 1957. I was writing music that would get you kicked out of church, because in those days, if you wanted to sing in a church you couldn't do it with a guitar. In the Bible Belt we had a piano – an upright, out-of-tune piano. And the choir sang, but you couldn't come in there and make any music that had a little tempo.

Then there were these other people who were offering me a whole lot of money, treating me like a hero, singing my songs. I got into rock and roll and suddenly all of my heroes were helping me make albums, and I was helping them make albums – the Beatles, the Rolling Stones, The Who, Eric Clapton, Bob Dylan.

There were lots of opportunities and I just wasn't spiritually mature enough to handle that. By the time I came to Jesus I was addicted to heroin and cocaine; I was so strung out on drugs.

Everybody in rock 'n' roll took drugs. I only knew two people who didn't take drugs in 21 years in rock 'n' roll and both of them were alcoholics. When you're a kid, you think if you get to where you can have a Ferrari, sell a million records, earn enough money to go where you want and do what you want, you think you're going to be happy. But then you get there and nobody is happy. Everybody is depressed. And the marriages aren't working because nobody is really in love. They're all just using each other.

But then I got born again. I realized that God is love, and without Him there is nothing. I surrendered my life for the first time. I didn't just give God my problems and the stuff I was ashamed of and my sins, I gave Him my hopes and dreams, my relationships. God said to me, "I will fix anything you give Me total control of, or I'll replace it with something better."

Through this process of walking with God and learning how to trust Him in everything, I discovered that the blessings of God are exponential – they grow and expand daily. It's not about being all religious; it's just about treating God like He's God. And if you'll give Him a chance, He'll raise the quality of your life every single day.

Mylon LeFevre is a Christian singer/songwriter who got his start writing a hit song for Elvis Presley.

PRAYER

Father, I don't know how to be the Lord of my own life. I've messed up everything. I've ignored Your Word. I don't really know You; I know a little bit about You, I've sung about You, but I want to really know You. Come into my life and let me walk with You.

FURTHER STUDY

Psalm 34:8; Jeremiah 29:14; Matthew 7:7

A sign of weakness

"... human anger does not produce the righteousness that God desires." (James 1:20)

as a youngster, I had a horrible temper.

Once, a fellow hit me with a pebble. It didn't hurt, but I was incensed that he would dare hit me. So I picked up a large rock, hurled it at his face and broke his glasses.

Another fellow tried to get me to close my locker. I didn't want it closed. So I struck him in the forehead with my fist, with the lock still in my hand, and put a three-inch gash in his forehead.

When I was 14, yet another youngster angered me. I had a large camping knife so I tried to stab him in the abdomen. Fortunately, he had on a large metal belt buckle under his clothing and the knife blade struck it with such force that it broke and he fled in terror. But I was more horrified than he was and I locked myself in the bathroom for hours.

I realized with a temper like mine I would never see my dream of becoming a physician. I knew my options were jail, reform school, or the grave, and none of those appealed to me. So I just said, "Lord, You've got to help me. I cannot control my temper."

I picked up the Bible and opened it to the book of Proverbs. There were all these verses in there about fools, and it looked like they all described me.

Then there were verses about anger:

A hot-tempered person must pay the penalty; rescue them, and you will have to do it again.
(Proverbs 19:19)

Better a patient person than a warrior, one with self-control than one who takes a city. (Proverbs 16:32)

I realized while I was in that bathroom that to punch somebody, or to kick down a door, was not a sign of strength; it was a sign of weakness. It meant that you were easily manipulated by the environment and by other people, and that you were, of all people, the weakest if you were the angriest.

When I came out of that bathroom, after three hours, the temper was gone. I've never had another problem with it since that time. Some people say, "Well, you just learned how to hide it." But I've got to tell you, when the Lord fixes it, He doesn't just paint it over. He fixes it from the inside.

Dr. Ben Carson is a neurosurgeon and the author of *America the Beautiful*.

PRAYER

Lord, take my weakness and exchange it for Your strength. Fill me with whatever is good and pure and lovely. Fix me from the inside, so that in all ways I would glorify You.

FURTHER STUDY

Psalm 37:8; Proverbs 22:24; Ephesians 4:31; 1 Peter 3:4

Take me to the place

Instead of your shame you will receive a double portion, and instead of disgrace you will rejoice in your inheritance. And so you will inherit a double portion in your land, and everlasting joy will be yours. (Isaiah 61:7)

between the ages of five and nine I was abused by several different people who told me to never say a word. And I carried that shame that I couldn't talk about into my adult life, a shame so deep I never thought I would deserve the kind of love my heart desired.

Then one night, a stranger approached me and told me everything about my life that I had never spoken to another human being, only the things that God and I knew. And I cried like I don't think I will ever cry again in my life.

The stranger said, "Now that you have emptied yourself of all of that junk, I'm going to pray that God's presence fills every crevice and every crack." And that night, God supernaturally changed my life forever.

When God told me it was time to share my story with others, He led me to the story of Lazarus in John chapter 11. As I got to the part where Mary meets Jesus and she says, "If You would have been here my brother would still be alive," I instantly had flashbacks of myself as a young girl.

I knew the Word of God said that He would never leave me nor forsake me, that He would be with me even until the end, that He had plans for a future and a hope. But that young girl was crying out, "Jesus, if You would have been there . . . If You are what Your Word says You are . . . How could You allow that to happen to me?"

Jesus responds to Mary by saying, "Where have you laid him?" Another translation says, "Take me to the place where you have laid him."

God was telling me that I had to take Christ to the place that I had hidden, the place where my innocence, my purity, all of those hopes and dreams had died. So that He could take away all my shame.

The whole purpose of Lazarus' story was for God's glory to be revealed. And, like Mary and Lazarus, I know the glory of God because of what I went through. I don't know why people have to face things. But I do know that He can wash away all of the pain and shame we carry.

Whatever you have faced, don't be afraid. Take Jesus to that place, and He will heal you there.

Amanda Crabb is a singer/songwriter and praise leader, together with her husband Aaron, for Cornerstone Church in San Antonio, Texas.

PRAYER

Jesus, raise me to new life. Forgive me, cleanse me, take away the hurt, the shame, the past, blot it out – just give me a new beginning. Jesus, come to that place.

FURTHER STUDY

Deuteronomy 31:6; Isaiah 54:4; Jeremiah 29:11; John 11

The issue of forgiveness

Be kind and compassionate to one another, forgiving each other, just as in Christ God forgave you. (Ephesians 4:32)

There's no greater issue that people grapple with than the issue of forgiveness. "How can I know how to forgive somebody who has hurt me?"

Someone reading this right now has been deeply hurt by another person. It may be a mate who had an affair or a friend who wronged you in some way. You can't move any further in life until you deal with this issue of forgiveness.

There may be an abused wife right now reading this who knows she's supposed to forgive but she thinks, *Does that mean I have to go back and live with this abusive mate?* Returning to your mate isn't forgiveness; that would be reconciliation. So one reason people have such a hard time with forgiveness is they really have a misunderstanding about what forgiveness is and what it isn't.

When I forgive somebody, what I'm doing is giving up my right to hurt them for hurting me. I give up my right to vengeance. I don't give up my desire for justice; I'm turning them over to God to let God deal with them. But I'm letting go so I can get on with my life.

The biggest mistake Christians make about forgiveness is trying to make our forgiveness dependent on what the other person does or doesn't do. We are waiting for them to apologize or change so we can forgive. Or we think they need to acknowledge our forgiveness in some way.

But in Mark 11:25, Jesus said, *"And when you stand praying, if you hold anything against anyone, forgive them, so that your Father in heaven may forgive you your sins."* Jesus was saying you have the ability – whether that person is in the same room, the next room, the next state, or in the cemetery – to forgive.

When you refuse to forgive somebody, you are emotionally binding yourself to that other person. And you can't go any further or faster in life than he or she is willing to go. But forgiveness is the process by which I let go of that person. I say what that person did to me is wrong, they deserve to suffer for it, but I'm letting go of that hurt so I can be free to get on with my life.

Lewis Smedes once said, "To forgive is to set a prisoner free and discover that the prisoner was you."

Dr. Robert Jeffress is pastor of First Baptist Church, Dallas, Texas, and author of *How Can I Know? Answers to 7 of Life's Most Important Questions.*

PRAYER

Father, help me be quick to forgive those who offend or wrong me. I know that it will do my heart good to be free from anger, resentment and unforgiveness. Lord, if there is anyone I need to forgive right now, bring them to my remembrance so I can let go of that hurt and get on with my life.

FURTHER STUDY

Matthew 6:9-15; Matthew 18:21-22; Luke 6:37; Colossians 3:13

On the way down

The blessing of the LORD makes one rich, and He adds no sorrow with it. (Proverbs 10:22, NKJV)

my wife and I started with nothing. When we were 22 years old, we got married, and we were broke. We were eating off a card table and driving a 1902 Pinto. By the time I was 26 years old, I started buying and selling real estate. I had about $4 million worth of real estate, but I hadn't been smart about it. I had way too much debt.

It all looked good, but it wasn't real. So when my bank got sold to another bank they said, "This kid owes us two million." And they wanted to limit the relationship, which is banker talk for "ruin my life."

I didn't grow up knowing God. I met Him on the way up, but I really got to know Him on the way down.

We spent the next two and a half years losing everything we owned. We were sued and we were foreclosed on. And finally, with a newborn and a toddler and a marriage hanging on by a thread, we were bankrupt.

There were some men stepping into the Evangelical space at that time teaching people God's Word and what it says about money. So, with nothing else available to me, I started studying the Bible.

My wife and I started applying God's principles to our lives. It took a while. I'd like to say we bounced back immediately, but we didn't. We sat around and blamed everybody else for a while. But we slowly began to heal and take ownership of our mistakes. Then people were attracted to that. It's like when your good friend loses a bunch of weight you say, "How did you do that?"

People would say to us, "How did y'all not kill each other? How did y'all stay married? How did you get back up to where you could walk again?" because everybody knew we were knocked flat.

We started sharing the 2500 Scriptures God had pointed us to regarding His view on possessions, and the things you're supposed to do to handle money properly. And we came to see these not as strict principles, but just our heavenly Father who is crazy about us saying, "I love you. I want you to have a good life. This is how you live."

Dave Ramsey is the author of *Financial Peace*, and coauthor, with his daughter Rachel Cruze, of *Smart Money Smart Kids*. *The Dave Ramsey Show* is a nationally syndicated radio show with over six million listeners.

PRAYER

Lord, You are the Father on the throne. I am Your inheritance; I'm Your heir. You have given me all the principles I need to live a successful life, free from the burden of poverty and lack. Thank You for the abundant life available in You.

FURTHER STUDY

Proverbs 22:6; Matthew 6:24; Luke 14:28–30; 1 John 3:17

More than enough

Now to Him who is able to do exceedingly abundantly above all that we ask or think, according to the power that works in us, to Him be glory . . . forever and ever. Amen. (Ephesians 3:20–21, NKJV)

I hear all the time about God answering prayer and working in other people's lives. But you can believe it for other people, and still not believe it for yourself.

I found there was a disconnect in my life. I celebrated the testimonies of what God had done for others, but at the exact same time there were some things in my own life I couldn't bring myself to pray about. I was too nervous about putting it out there just in case God chose, in His sovereignty, not to answer it the way I had requested.

John chapter two includes the story of Jesus changing water into wine. Even though Mary is not directly involved, she is the only one who is willing to come out and say, "Jesus, we've got a problem."

I think sometimes He is just waiting on that admission. Because as soon as Mary enlisted Jesus, was willing to be open and authentic about the issue they were having, all of a sudden they had more than they could even share with all of the guests, and it was the best wine that they had ever tasted before. Mary didn't ask for the best wine. She didn't ask for more than enough. She was simply honest about the need and invited Jesus to do something about it.

Jesus really does do exceedingly, abundantly, beyond for us. He doesn't just do what you ask, He does beyond what you can ever ask or imagine. Which means we sell ourselves short when we want Him to answer our requests exactly the way we ask. Because our brains can't even touch the fringe of His ability in our life.

I've learned to trust God, to come to Him and pray out loud the things that I desire, not holding back in fear and trepidation, worried that what is important to me is not also important to Him. But I've also gained a quiet confidence that when God says "no," or when He says, "wait," or when He answers the request in a completely different way, I can just sit back, rest easy, and know that God's got my back. And if this is the answer that He's chosen, that means that this is the best possible conclusion.

Priscilla Shirer, a gifted communicator, is the author of several bestselling books, including *God is Able*.

PRAYER

Lord, I trust You to know what is best for me. Thank You for exceeding my wildest dreams, my deepest longings, for hearing my prayer and reminding me over and over of Your abundant grace, mercy and love.

FURTHER STUDY

Psalm 46:10; Psalm 62:5; John 2:1–12

Jesus at the center

Dear friends, let us love one another, for love comes from God. Everyone who loves has been born of God and knows God. (1 John 4:7)

i was right out of high school when a lady started living with my mom and me. After a couple months, my mom admitted to me that they were partners.

That was difficult for me. I was so immature and legalistic. I was the kid who didn't smoke, didn't drink, didn't have sex, therefore I believed I was better than you. Now I would never say that. But it's the attitude and the spirit, similar to the Pharisees, that I had.

I know now I wasn't even really a Christian then. I would have claimed it, but I didn't "get" Jesus.

At that point I felt bitterness, even hatred toward my mom and her choices. And that led me down a rebellious lifestyle. But it too was insufficient. It didn't fulfill me any more than "following the rules" did.

So now I had lived a "religious" lifestyle and I'd lived a "rebellious" lifestyle, and it just seemed like that couldn't be all there was. There had to be something more. I found Jesus at the center of that.

My mom and I disagree. But we love each other. And that's the life Jesus wants us to live.

America prides itself on being a pluralistic nation, meaning there are a bunch of different voices, religions, etc. But that's not true. True pluralism is when every voice has a voice in the marketplace and every voice is saying, "Let's set our differences aside and start pursuing truth."

But what we have is tribalism. Tribalism is where you go to your tribe and I go to mine; you retreat and you throw your rocks trying to stone the "other" people.

Because of social media, my generation is absolutely terrified of real community. The biblical definition of community involves being transparent and honest and vulnerable – almost like a spiritual nakedness where someone can see all that you are, they know your failures, shortcomings, hurts, shame, guilt, differences and they still want you and they still say, "I love you; I know you."

True community is the love that my mom and I have for one another, our willingness to listen to and respect one another. I hope we can be a microcosm of the culture we want to create.

Jefferson Bethke is the author of *Jesus > Religion: Why He is So Much Better than Trying Harder, Doing More, and Being Good Enough.* His YouTube video, "Why I Hate Religion, But Love Jesus," has over 27 million views.

PRAYER

Heavenly Father, help me create a culture of love and reconciliation in my community. Show me where I need to let go of condemnation and open my heart to ALL of Your children, especially those I disagree with. Thank You for sending Your Son to teach us how to love.

FURTHER STUDY

Luke 6; 2 Corinthians 5:18; Revelation 3:20

A transformed life

Taste and see that the LORD is good; blessed is the one who takes refuge in him. (Psalm 34:8)

i was born again when I was eight years old. Growing up I never said a word of profanity, never took a drink of liquor, never smoked a cigarette. I loved the Lord and I was living the Christian life as I was told, yet there was zero power and zero victory in my life.

Then the Lord showed up on March 23, 1968, and transformed my life. I didn't understand a lot but I felt the presence of God. For four and a half months I was caught up in the presence of God; I was gone someplace. But when I finally came back down to earth, nobody wanted me. I was too radical for the church. When I finally became usable, they didn't want me anymore, because when we don't understand something we fear it or try to stop it.

So the best thing that ever happened to me was getting drafted and sent to Vietnam. That was my Bible college. For over a year in Vietnam, I spent anywhere from 12–15 hours a day studying the Word, and it transformed my life.

I had been born again, and I was loving God and serving Him the best I knew how, but boy, what I didn't know was killing me. And when I began to learn these truths through God's Word, it totally turned my life around.

I feel like God has called me to be a teacher of the Word, not so much to inspire people to come to the Lord, but to see people who know the Lord and yet don't know the goodness of what He's done for us; I have a passion to see them receive that.

I believe there are a lot of people who love God but are doing their own thing and asking God to bless it. Since I found out what God has called me to do, I've never asked God to bless what I'm doing. If God tells me to do it, I know it is blessed. It's so much easier to find what He wants you to do and just do it. There's a blessing and an anointing you don't have when you're doing your own thing.

The best thing, the thing we need to utterly depend on, is the Word of God and the Truth setting people free.

Andrew Wommack is a Bible teacher, reaching millions of people through daily *Gospel Truth* radio and television broadcasts.

PRAYER

Lord, I want to know You more deeply, understand Your love more completely, be used by You more fully. Put the desire in my heart to spend more time in Your Word, experiencing You and all You have for me.

FURTHER STUDY

Isaiah 40:31; Romans 12:2; Colossians 3:16

Get off the train

Do not conform to the pattern of this world, but be transformed by the re-newing of your mind. Then you will be able to test and approve what God's will is – his good, pleasing and perfect will. (Romans 12:2)

When I was at Sydney University, I lived in a city called Seven Hills. I would catch a train from Seven Hills to Sydney University, and it would be a 45 minute train trip each way every day. It left every day from platform four at 7:30 in the morning. I would do it like clockwork.

This one day, I arrived at the station. It was 7:30, platform four, and a train was waiting about to depart. I bolted down the stairs just as the train doors were closing. I jumped in the middle of the train doors and got on just in time. I was exhilarated!

Now, the train I'm supposed to be on travels 45 minutes in one direction. So I knew I was in trouble when the train immediately began to move in the opposite direction. I had caught an express train to Katoomba, to the Blue Mountains. So instead of going 45 minutes in the right direction, I was then on an hour express going the opposite direction.

When we arrived in Katoomba, I got off the train, looked at the station master, threw up my hands and said, "How did I get here?!"

And he said, "Well love, you got on the wrong train, didn't you?"

That's exactly what we're like at the end of many days. We get there and we say, "God, how did I get here?"

And God says, "Honey, you just got on the wrong train of thought."

Because our thoughts are like a train because they take us somewhere.

I had so many wrong thought patterns in the past. I thought so many wrong thoughts. I would jump on the wrong train of thought every day and I still can do that if I'm not careful; that's why I have to get the Word of God into me first thing in the morning.

I promise you, before you wake up in the morning the devil will make sure that the wrong trains of thoughts are coming into the platform of your mind. But just because it comes into the platform doesn't mean you have to jump on that train of thought. You need to check the destination board before you get on the train. And do you know what? If you get on the wrong train, just jump off! That's one train you're allowed to jump off of.

Christine Caine is cofounder, with her husband Nick, of the A21 Campaign to fight human trafficking. A native of Australia, she is the author of several books including *Undaunted: Daring to do What God Calls You to do.*

PRAYER

Father, I am who You say I am and I have what You say I have. You say I have the mind of Christ, and with that knowledge I will take every thought captive, renewing my mind daily, in order to honor You.

FURTHER STUDY

Proverbs 23:7; Luke 10:27; 1 Corinthians 2:16; 2 Corinthians 10:5

The gospel of grace

For it is by grace you have been saved, through faith – and this is not from yourselves, it is the gift of God . . . (Ephesians 2:8–9)

forgive me for saying this, but America needs the Gospel.

I thank God America has been the number one nation to send missionaries out in years past and I'm a beneficiary of that; Singapore is a beneficiary of that, Malaysia, Vietnam, Cambodia, even China; there's a large underground church, a large army of believers all over Asia now, even Korea is a beneficiary of the presence of the Americans there and the missionaries.

But right now we feel like God is sending missionaries to America because they have forgotten what the Gospel is all about. They feel that the Gospel is another disguise for the law to come forth. Americans believe that when you do good, you get good; when you do bad, you get bad. But that's not what grace is all about.that's not the Gospel. The Gospel is you can receive good you don't deserve because another received all the bad that you deserved. Now that takes the Holy Spirit to elucidate. Any religion can teach do good to get good, do bad to get bad.

It takes the Holy Spirit to elucidate on the beauties of Jesus, His glories, His excellences and how God has set Him to your account. God sees you in Him. And that's the Gospel of Jesus Christ; that God made Him who knew no sin to become sin for us that we who knew no righteousness might be made the righteousness of God in Him. That's the Gospel.

The founding fathers were not averse to using the name Jesus in their writings. What made them great leaders is that they believed the Gospel. They believed the Gospel of grace. They believed in the Lord Jesus Christ as their righteousness. That's what produced godly character in them. That's what produced the wisdom and intelligence by which they governed this nation.

But now we want the character, we want the integrity, we want the wisdom in our leaders without the Gospel. We're preaching right living, right living, right living, but there's very little right living. The intention is right, but we've got to preach the Gospel, and the Gospel is not just for a one-time salvation experience but for life.

Joseph Prince, pastor from New Creation Church, Singapore, is the author of *The Power Of Right Believing*.

PRAYER

Lord, I pray for America right now. I pray that we will reclaim Your Gospel, the Gospel of grace. Thank You for showing us mercy where we fall short, for sending Your Son to take our place on the Cross, for igniting this passion for revitalization in America today. We know that with You all things are possible to those who believe.

FURTHER STUDY

Isaiah 61; Matthew 5:17; Acts 20:24; Ephesians 3:7

Freedom is for you

The LORD gives freedom to the prisoners. (Psalm 146:7, NKJV)

have you ever felt insecure? Been afraid to fail? Felt plain and ordinary when others around you seem to be shining stars?

Do you think you have to be "good" for God to love you? You have to "do" in order to be someone? You don't measure up to others? You're ugly, invisible, or inadequate?

If any of these secret thoughts apply to you, I want you to know that you're not alone. But it can certainly feel that way. I know, because I have struggled personally with every single one of those things.

For years I lived in a prison of fear and self-doubt, paralyzed by the false thinking that God would love me only if I was good, which to me translated to being busy "doing something" for Him. And yet no matter what I did, it was never enough. I was still plain, ordinary Betty – the middle, invisible, inadequate child who grew up feeling like she never measured up.

I'm here to tell you that Jesus took me from the shackles of fear to true freedom. Although the journey has taken me many years, and it's not entirely over yet (because He is continually refining me), I can now boldly say that I finally have discovered the "good news:" God loves us and accepts us just as we are, right now.

We don't have to be perfect to come before him. He is waiting for us, longing for intimate, two-way conversation. And He longs to show us how to break out of our individual prisons – negative thoughts, addictions, destructive patterns – He wants us free!

Free to be the unique people He has created us to be. And, most of all, free to pursue, without hindrance, the kind of loving relationship He longs to have with us as His children.

So today, ask Him for freedom in every area of your life. He will give it to you!

Betty Robison cohosts *LIFE TODAY* with her husband, James. The Robisons are also founders of LIFE Outreach International, a worldwide ministry and missions organization.

PRAYER

Father, I thank You for the freedom You have given me in Christ Jesus. I want to walk in that freedom in every single area of my life. I want to experience freedom in my relationships, my finances and in my day-to-day struggles. I want to be free to love others as You love them. I ask to experience Your freedom in a new way today.

FURTHER STUDY

2 Corinthians 3:17; John 8:36

One nation, under God

Arise! For this matter is your responsibility, but we will be with you; be courageous and act. (Ezra 10:4, NASB)

When I was in my mid-30s, Billy Graham called a prayer meeting. About 10 of us gathered. Billy said, "We've only got 1000 days of freedom left in America unless the Soviet ideology and military aggression are defeated. We've got to pray. We've got to have principled leadership – not just people who talk religion, but principled leadership that can communicate with conviction what needs to happen."

A few others and I said, "We'll lay our lives down to speak truth to this nation."

We hosted a prayer meeting in Washington in the spring called "Washington for Jesus," and nearly a million people came together. God then led me to call the National Affairs Briefing and invite all the presidential candidates. Against the advice of his advisors, one said he would come: Mr. Ronald Reagan.

Mr. Reagan was so far down in the polls at the time of the National Affairs Briefing that there was no way he could have been elected. But after what happened there, the pendulum swung.

Mr. Reagan gave us hope for America that night; he emphasized our role and God's role. He said:

Since the start of my presidential campaign, many others and I have felt a new vitality in American politics; a fresh sense of purpose, a deeper feeling of commitment is giving new energy and new direction to our public life. You are the reason. Religious America is awakening perhaps just in time for our country's sake. I've seen the impact of your dedication. I know the sincerity of your intent and I'm deeply honored to be with you here tonight. I'm told that throughout history, man has adopted about four billion laws. It always seems to me however, that in all that time with all those laws we haven't improved one iota on the Ten Commandments.

The media reported that 17,000 people attended the briefing and 50 million were impacted by what hap-

---

James Robison is cohost of *LIFE TODAY* with his wife of more than 50 years, Betty. The Robisons are also founders of LIFE Outreach International, a worldwide ministry and missions organization.

pened there – the whole community of faith. A miracle of God happened and it wasn't because of a party, it wasn't even because of a person, it was because of the power of prayer and a return to godly principles.

As Christians we can participate in whatever political party we want to, actively, but it is our responsibility to keep pointing that party and its candidates to the principles and standards of God.

PRAYER

God, I have a broken heart for America, a nation in desperate need of healing. Heal our land, our nation, the Church, Lord. Remind us that we are one nation, under God, and as such we each have a responsibility for the future of this great nation.

FURTHER STUDY

Hosea 4:6; Matthew 5:13–16